"Practice Makes Perfect"

CONTENTS PAGE

Think Smart Academy ltd ©

ADDITION

Work out the following questions and write your answer in the space provided.

1.

48 + 23 =

2.

34 + 69 =

3.

52 + 47 =

4.

73 + 52 =

5.

105 + 64 =

6.

394 + 214 =

7.

323 + 49 =

8.

482 + 463 =

9.

1232 + 954 =

10.

12433 + 31729 =

SUBTRACTION

Work out the following questions and write your answer in the space provided.

11.

29 - 13 =

12.

67 - 38 =

13.

57 - 19 =

14.

71 - 58 =

15.

136 - 78 =

16.

232 - 88 =

17.

423 - 174 =

18.

947 - 359 =

19.

1594 - 945 =

20.

3462 - 1795 =

MULTIPLICATION

Work out the following questions and write your answer in the space provided.

21.

14 x 9 =

22.

16 x 5 =

23.

23 x 13 =

24.

35 x 11 =

25.

44 x 16 =

26.

95 x 22 =

27.

159 x 13 =

28.

248 x 71 =

29.

405 x 62 =

30.

512 x 108 =

DIVISION

Work out the following questions and write your answer in the space provided.

31.

84 ÷ 6 =

32.

180 ÷ 12 =

33.

$312 \div 8 =$

34.

$564 \div 12 =$

35.

$696 \div 24 =$

36.

$595 \div 35 =$

37.

$1539 \div 81 =$

38.

$1848 \div 33 =$

39.

$1562 \div 71 =$

40.

$3686 \div 97 =$

BODMAS

Work out the answer for the following questions and circle the correct answer from the multiple choices provided.

41.

4 + 3 x 6 =

A: 42

B: 22

C: 44

D: 20

E: 26

42.

9 - 4 x 5 =

A: 24

B: 25

C: -11

D: -12

E: 18

43.

7 + 12 x 2 =

A: 31

B: 38

C: 30

D: 37

E: 39

44.

7 x 5 – 3 + 2 =

A: 16

B: 0

C: 7

D: 30

E: 34

Think Smart Academy ltd ©

45.

5 + (4 x 3) x 2 =

A: 54

B: 34

C: 29

D: 18

E: 15

46.

13 – 12 + (11 – 9) =

A: -1

B: -9

C: 1

D: -11

E: 0

47.

(9 x 3) + (4 x 8) =

A: 504

B: 252

C: 61

D: 59

E: 128

48.

26 - (5 x 9) - 15 =

A: 175

B: -34

C: 174

D: 173

E: 34

49.

$13 + (6 \times 4) \div 2$

A: 38

B: 18.5

C: 19

D: 26

E: 25

50.

$8 - 7 + (4 \times 8) + 15 =$

A: -19

B: -18

C: -46

D: 49

E: -17

51.

$(20 \div 4) - 7 + 6 =$

A: 6

B: 9

C: -4

D: 3

E: -8

52.

$6 \times 7 - 3 \times 8 =$

A: 18

B: 19

C: 312

D: 320

E: 308

Think Smart Academy ltd ©

53.

13 − 6 x 8 + 12 =

A: -22

B: 68

C: 69

D: 70

E: -47

54.

6 x 8 + (13 x 2) ÷ 2 =

A: 70

B: 61

C: 63

D: 44

E: 37

55.

47 + 8 - 5 - (12 x 2) x 2 =

A: 52

B: 5

C: 104

D: 8

E: 2

56.

31 + (9 x 6) x 3 =

A: 720

B: 193

C: 710

D: 730

E: 190

57.

31 + 8 - 12 - (8 x 6) =

A: -21

B: 111

C: 109

D: 112

E: -23

58.

42 x 1 - 2 - (6 x 6) x 4 =

A: -109

B: 674

C: -104

D: 692

E: 109

59.

25 x 2 - 13 - (3 x 9) x 2 =

A: 20

B: 482

C: -17

D: 15

E: 17

60.

Calculate $18 - (4 \times 2^2) \div 2$

A: 10

B: 1

C: 2

D: 20

E: 5

Think Smart Academy ltd ©

PLACE VALUE

Work out the answer for the following questions and circle the correct answer from the multiple choices provided.

61.

Which digit is in the tens value of 35049?

A: 3

B: 5

C: 0

D: 4

E: 9

62.

Which digit is in the hundreds value of 42196?

A: 4

B: 2

C: 1

D: 9

E: 6

63.

Which digit is in the thousands value of 75924?

A: 7

B: 5

C: 9

D: 2

E: 4

64.

Which digit is in the tens value of 432.61?

A: 4

B: 3

C: 2

D: 6

E: 1

65.

Which digit is in the thousandths value of 49126.7258?

A: 1

B: 9

C: 2

D: 5

E: 8

66.

Which digit is in the ten thousands value of 294,318?

A: 2

B: 9

C: 4

D: 3

E: 1

67.

Which digit is in the hundred thousands value of 816,435?

A: 8

B: 1

C: 6

D: 4

E: 3

68.

Which digit is in the tens value of 9203.7?

A: 9

B: 2

C: 0

D: 3

E: 7

69.

Which digit is in the tenths value of 251.68?

A: 2

B: 5

C: 1

D: 6

E: 8

70.

Which digit is in the hundreds value of 791.42?

A: 7

B: 9

C: 1

D: 4

E: 2

71.

What is the value of 1 tenth added to 190.02?

A: 191.02

B: 190.03

C: 1900.2

D: 200.02

E: 190.12

72.

What is the value of 209.58 minus 10?

A: 199.58

B: 212.58

C: 219.58

D: 209.58

E: 199.42

73.

What is the value of 4 hundredths added to 219.67?

A: 219.70

B: 220.67

C: 220.17

D: 219.71

E: 224.67

74.

What is the value of 7 tenths added to 199.52?

A: 200.02

B: 201.22

C: 1900.2

D: 200.22

E: 190.12

75.

1000 people buy tickets for a concert at a cost of £185.60 per ticket. How much money is made by the concert in total?

A: £185600

B: £18.56

C: £18560

D: £185.60

E: £190.12

76.

The number 165.82 is doubled. What is the value of the answer's units column?

A: 9

B: 2

C: 5

D: 7

E: 1

77.

The cost of taking a taxi is £5.67 per mile. A man takes a taxi 100 miles. What is the value of the total cost's tens column?

A: 5

B: 7

C: 0

D: 6

E: 1

78.

The total cost of a dinner is £1208. It is shared equally between 50 people. What is the value of the number in the tenths column of the amount paid per person?

A: 8

B: 2

C: 1

D: 7

E: 6

79.

Replace the X's below with the numbers 2,3,4,5,7 and 8 to make the statement correct:

XX + XX = XX

A: 25 + 48 = 73

B: 32 + 45 = 87

C: 57 + 83 = 24

D: 28 + 52 = 70

E: 73 + 42 = 84

80.

How many odd three digit numbers can be made from the digits 2, 5 and 7? You may only use each digit once.

A: 2

B: 3

C: 4

D: 9

E: 5

Work out the answer for the following questions and circle the correct answer from the multiple choices provided.

81.

$3.4 + 7.2 = ?$.

A: 10.6

B: 10.8

C: 9.6

D: 11.6

E: 11.8

82.

$5.9 + 6.8 = ?$.

A: 11.7

B: 12.5

C: 13.7

D: 12.9

E: 12.7

83.

$7.5 - 3.9 = ?$

A: 4.6

B: 3.8

C: 3.6

D: 3.4

E: 4.4

84.

$8.4 \div 3 = ?$

A: 2.6

B: 3.4

C: 1.8

D: 2.8

E: 3.2

85.

2.5 x 1.5 = ?

A: 3.5

B: 3.75

C: 3.85

D: 4

E: 3.95

86.

4.05 x 3 = ?

A: 12.15

B: 12.5

C: 12.25

D: 12.35

E: 12.5

87.

Which of these numbers is the greatest?

6.0909, 6.0108, 6.0834, 6.0099, 6.0910

A: 6.0909

B: 6.0108

C: 6.0834

D: 6.0099

E: 6.0910

88.

Which of these numbers is the least?

90.0129, 90.0190, 90.0139, 90.0120, 90.0210

A: 90.0129

B: 90.0190

C: 90.0139

D: 90.0120

E: 90.0210

89.

Which of these numbers is the most?

42, 42.00902, 42.000199, 42.00901, 42.00029

A: 42

B: 42.00902

C: 42.000199

D: 42.00901

E: 42.00029

90.

Calculate 402.34 x 100

A: 4,023.4

B: 40,234

C: 402,340

D: 40.234

E: 36

91.

Calculate 402.34 x 0.1

A: 4,023.4

B: 40,234

C: 402,340

D: 40.234

E: 36

92.

What is the value of 209.58 minus 10?

A: 199.58

B: 212.58

C: 219.58

D: 209.58

E: 199.42

93.

How many tenths are there between 141.7 and 143.5?

A: 18

B: 13

C: 10

D: 9

E: 8

94.

A number machine takes the number in the units column of its input and multiplies it by the number in the hundredths column. What is the output of the number machine when its input is 25.67?

A: 12

B: 14

C: 35

D: 30

E: 10

95.

If 81.2 x 45 = 3654, what is 0.812 x 450?

A: 365.4

B: 36.54

C: 450

D: 36540

E: 0.3654

96.

If 61.3 x 89 = 5455.7, what is 5455.7 ÷ 0.89?

A: 61300

B: 61.3

C: 0.613

D: 6130

E: 545570

DECIMALS

97.

Renting a car costs £23.47 upfront plus £12.47 per day. If Shyanne rents a car for 4 days and wants to pay the cost in only 1 pence pieces, how many will they need?

A: 7335

B: 733.5

C: 73.35

D: 0.7335

E: 73350

98.

If 42 / 0.75 = 56, what is 42 x 750?

A: 56000

B: 560

C: 56

D: 31500

E: 5.6

99.

Stephen has a number. He halves the digit in the tenths column then adds one point seven and ends up with 3.249, what number did he start with?

A: 2.359

B: 1.589

C: 1.764

D: 3.249

E: 1.673

100.

The value C x 0.10 = 482.3 and the value D x 100 = 0.3. What is the value of C + D?

A: 48.2303

B: 4823.003

C: 4823.03

D: 482.303

E: 482.033

Work out the answer for the following questions and circle the correct answer from the multiple choices provided.

101.

I go to the shops and buy 3 rolls at £2.50 each plus a magazine at £4.25. How much do I spend in total?

A: £12.05

B: £12.15

C: £11.50

D: £11.75

E: £12.75

102.

I go to the shops with a £10 note and buy four packets of tissues at £1.05 each. How much change do I get back?

A: £5.90

B: £6.05

C: £5.80

D: £5.85

E: £5.75

103.

Steve has a £20 note and buys 4 packets of crisps. If he receives £16.80 change, how much was 1 packet of crisps?

A: £3.20

B: 40p

C: £1.20

D: 80p

E: 90p

104.

A family of 2 adults and 4 children paid a total of £54 to go to the safari park. If a child ticket was £6, how much was an adult ticket?

A: £10

B: £15

C: £12.50

D: £22

E: £21

105.

Jacob decides to save all his 5p pieces in a money box. He ends up with £2.40. How many 5p pieces did he save?

A: 60

B: 46

C: 42

D: 48

E: 50

106.

Carole went to the shops and bought 5 loaves of bread and 5 bottles of water. If one loaf of bread cost 50p and 1 bottle of water costs £1.50, how much change does she get back from £10?

A: 50p

B: 0

C: £1.50

D: 75p

E: £1

107.

A crate holds 26 packets of orange juice. If four crates cost £52, what is the cost of one packet of orange juice?

A: 50p

B: £1

C: £1.50

D: 75p

E: £1.25

108.

Jim has saved £325 towards a new games console. The console was £450 but has been reduced by 20% in a sale. How much more does Jim need to save in order to buy the console at the sale price?

A: £30

B: £35

C: £40

D: £45

E: £50

109.

9 children each had an equal share of a sum of money. They each received £2.68 and there was 8p left over. How much was the original sum of money?

A: £25

B: £24.12

C: £24.20

D: £23.88

E: £24.50

110.

At the shop, pens cost £1.50 for a pack and rubbers cost 50p for a pack. In the sale, a pack of pens has been reduced by a fifth and a pack of rubbers by a tenth. How much would it now cost to buy 4 packs of pens and 3 packs of rubbers?

A: £6.35

B: £7

C: £5.75

D: £6.50

E: £6.15

111.

In 1975, £1 was worth the same as $2.20. How many pounds was $1,056 worth?

A: £440

B: £1,056

C: £480

D: £520

E: £2,323.20

112.

William and Sandra have some money. William had £13 more than Sandra. In total they £51. How much money does William have?

A: £38

B: £30

C: £31

D: £33

E: £32

113.

How many different ways are there of paying exactly £1 using 5p and / or 10p pieces?

A: 15

B: 10

C: 21

D: 11

E: 100

114.

How many tins of beans, worth 50p each, could you buy with a £10 note if the beans were discounted by 20%?

A: 20

B: 15

C: 18

D: 10

E: 25

115.

Latifa has £20 which she will share amongst her 4 children, Ada, Bo, Carrie, David. She gives 30% to Ada, 1/5 to Carrie, then Bo and David share the remainder equally. How much does David get?

A: £5

B: £8

C: £3

D: £10

E: £6

116.

Mo buys a car for £4000. Every year it loses 10% of its <u>present</u> value, how much will it be worth after 3 years?

A: £3921

B: £3300

C: £2916

D: £4000

E: £2800

117.

Three friends want to buy 7 pizzas for the best value. Shop 1 sells pizzas for £1.20 each, but with a 20% discount for purchases of more than 5 pizzas. Shop 2 sells pizzas for £1.80 with a 30% discount for orders of more than 5 pizzas. By how much is Shop 1 cheaper than Shop 2?

A: £4

B: £2.10

C: £7.10

D: £4.20

E: £2

118.

A box of 6 cans of cola costs £4.20. Each can holds 200ml of cola. A 1.5 litre bottle of cola costs £5. Which option is cheaper for buying 6 litres of cola and by how much?

A: Cans by £1

B: Bottles by £1

C: They're the same price

D: Cans by £2.50

E: Bottles by £5

119.

Together three friends, Fred, Gabby and Hannah, have £26. Gabby has 40% the amount of money that Fred has, Hannah has 20% more money than Fred. How much money does Gabby have?

A: £4

B: £10

C: £5

D: £12

E: £9

Think Smart Academy ltd ©

120.

I put £7.50 every two weeks into my savings account. How much will I have saved after 2 years?

A: £390

B: £780

C: £410

D: £380

E: £360

FRACTIONS

Work out the answer for the following questions and circle the correct answer from the multiple choices provided.

121.

What is a fifth of 60?

A: 5

B: 12

C: 20

D: 10

E: 15

122.

What is $\frac{5}{15}$ simplified as far as possible?

A: $\frac{1}{2}$

B: $\frac{1}{5}$

C: $\frac{3}{10}$

D: $\frac{1}{3}$

E: $\frac{2}{3}$

123.

What is $\frac{60}{75}$ simplified as far as possible?

A: $\frac{1}{2}$

B: $\frac{4}{5}$

C: $\frac{3}{10}$

D: $\frac{3}{5}$

E: $\frac{5}{6}$

124.

What is $\frac{5}{12}$ equivalent to?

A: $\frac{1}{2}$

B: $\frac{2}{5}$

C: $\frac{60}{144}$

D: $\frac{70}{144}$

E: $\frac{35}{60}$

125.

Calculate $\frac{1}{5} + \frac{1}{10}$

A: $\frac{1}{2}$

B: $\frac{1}{50}$

C: $\frac{3}{10}$

D: $\frac{2}{5}$

E: $\frac{2}{15}$

126.

Calculate $\frac{3}{7} + \frac{1}{10}$

A: $\frac{37}{70}$

B: $\frac{3}{5}$

C: $\frac{4}{17}$

D: $\frac{1}{2}$

E: $\frac{39}{70}$

127.

Calculate $\frac{4}{5} - \frac{2}{10}$

A: $\frac{3}{5}$

B: $\frac{1}{3}$

C: $\frac{2}{5}$

D: $\frac{1}{10}$

E: $\frac{1}{5}$

128.

Calculate $\frac{5}{9} - \frac{1}{3}$

A: $\frac{2}{5}$

B: $\frac{1}{3}$

C: $\frac{4}{9}$

D: $\frac{1}{3}$

E: $\frac{2}{9}$

129.

Calculate $\frac{5}{8} \div \frac{4}{5}$

A: $\frac{25}{32}$

B: $\frac{1}{2}$

C: $\frac{32}{25}$

D: $\frac{3}{4}$

E: $\frac{1}{3}$

130.

Calculate $\frac{2}{9} \div \frac{3}{7}$

A: $\frac{5}{63}$

B: $\frac{63}{5}$

C: $\frac{14}{27}$

D: $\frac{27}{14}$

E: $\frac{2}{3}$

131.

Calculate $\frac{2}{5} \times \frac{3}{7}$

A: $\frac{1}{2}$

B: $\frac{1}{3}$

C: $\frac{1}{4}$

D: $\frac{2}{35}$

E: $\frac{6}{35}$

132.

Calculate $\frac{4}{9} \times \frac{3}{5}$

A: $\frac{1}{3}$

B: $\frac{7}{45}$

C: $\frac{6}{15}$

D: $\frac{1}{4}$

E: $\frac{4}{15}$

133.

Calculate $2\frac{1}{5}$ x $4\frac{3}{5}$

A: $10\frac{2}{5}$

B: $10\frac{9}{25}$

C: $10\frac{1}{25}$

D: $10\frac{3}{25}$

E: $11\frac{3}{25}$

134.

Calculate $4\frac{2}{5}$ - $2\frac{2}{7}$

A: $2\frac{4}{35}$

B: $2\frac{8}{35}$

C: $2\frac{12}{35}$

D: $2\frac{1}{6}$

E: $2\frac{3}{7}$

135.

What is a fifth of a half of a sixth?

A: $\frac{1}{4}$

B: $\frac{1}{10}$

C: $\frac{1}{60}$

D: $\frac{1}{20}$

E: $\frac{1}{30}$

136.

Calculate $4\frac{2}{5} - 3\frac{1}{3}$

A: $1\frac{1}{2}$

B: $1\frac{2}{5}$

C: $\frac{1}{15}$

D: $1\frac{1}{15}$

E: $1\frac{1}{5}$

137.

A bus started off with 22 people on it. At stop A, half the people got off and 7 new people got on. At stop B, two thirds of the people on the bus got off and 2 people got on. How many people are now on the bus?

A: 8

B: 10

C: 5

D: 12

E: 14

138.

650 people are at the beach. A fifth of them are bare headed. Of the remainder, three quarters are wearing a hat and the rest are wearing a visor. How many are wearing a visor?

A: 130

B: 140

C: 120

D: 150

E: 160

139.

Two fifths of the 40 balls in the bag are blue. Of the rest, three quarters are red and the remainder yellow. How many yellow balls are there?

A: 4

B: 2

C: 8

D: 6

E: 10

140.

Richard eats two fifths of a pizza. Donna eats three quarters of a pizza. How much pizza have they eaten in total?

A: One and three fifths

B: Six twentieths

C: One and a half

D: One and three twentieths

E: One and two thirds

PERCENTAGES

Work out the answer for the following questions and circle the correct answer from the multiple choices provided.

141.

Calculate 40% of 600.

A: 240

B: 420

C: 400

D: 200

E: 500

142.

Calculate 20% of 700.

A: 180

B: 160

C: 140

D: 170

E: 200

143.

Calculate 40% of 2000.

A: 825

B: 900

C: 850

D: 750

E: 800

144.

What is four twentieths as a percentage?

A: 12%

B: 25%

C: 20%

D: 15%

E: 18%

145.

A quarter of the school year were born between January and March. If there are 200 pupils in the year, how many were born between April and December?

A: 50

B: 150

C: 140

D: 175

E: 180

146.

260 people are going to the beach. 70% of them are wearing a hat. How many are not wearing a hat?

A: 30

B: 120

C: 78

D: 182

E: 90

147.

Sid wants to buy a console in the sale. He has saved £165. The console was priced at £340 but has been reduced by 25% in the sale. How much more money will Sid need to save in order to buy the console in the sale?

A: £90

B: £100

C: £105

D: £85

E: £110

148.

Lucy's parents go to the shops with £250. They spend 40% on food and 30% on toiletries. How much money do they have left?

A: £175

B: £80

C: £85

D: £60

E: £75

Think Smart Academy ltd ©

149.

In a box of mixed fruit, there are 80 pieces. One fifth are lemons. 15% are oranges. The rest are apples. What percentage are apples?

A: 75%

B: 65%

C: 60%

D: 80%

E: 85%

150.

Which is the biggest of these values?

0.211   20%   0.029   21%   0.201

A: 0.211

B: 20%

C: 0.029

D: 21%

E: 0.201

151.

What is twenty-five percent of three hundred?

A: 100

B: 75

C: 30

D: 80

E: 70

152.

16,500 people go to the football match. 70% support the home team, 15% support the away team. The rest are neutral. How many people are neutral?

A: 2,775

B: 3,375

C: 2,500

D: 2,470

E: 2,475

Think Smart Academy ltd ©

153.

What is 65% as a fraction in its most simplified terms?

A: $\frac{1}{3}$
B: $\frac{13}{20}$
C: $\frac{4}{5}$
D: $\frac{5}{6}$
E: $\frac{5}{7}$

154.

Jane is drawing a pie chart of her survey results. She asked 300 people their favourite snacks. She draws a 120 degree angle for a slice called "Biscuits". How many people said their favourite snacks were Biscuits?

A: 120

B: 110

C: 80

D: 100

E: 105

155.

Dave leaves for school at 745am and arrives at 830am. Steve leaves at the same time but takes 20% longer to arrive at school. What time does Steve arrive at school?

A: 854am

B: 839am

C: 845am

D: 835am

E: 831am

156.

Krishan has £15,000 of savings. He has found a savings account that offers him 4% interest per year on the first £8,000 of savings and then 2% per year on everything above £8,000. What will be in his savings account at the end of the first year if he doesn't spend anything?

A: £15,320

B: £15,460

C: £15,430

D: £15,500

E: £15,400

157.

The coat in the sale was priced at £104. If the sale reduction was 20%, what was the original price of the coat?

A: £120

B: £112

C: £125

D: £140

E: £130

158.

The computer in the sale was originally priced at £550. Its first sale offer was 30% of the original price. The second sale offer was 40% of the original price. How much cheaper was the computer in the second sale offer than the first?

A: £50

B: £60

C: £55

D: £50.50

E: £55.50

159.

Peter got 80 marks in his exam which was 64%. How many marks were available in total?

A: 125

B: 100

C: 130

D: 120

E: 135

160.

The storage company realises that in order to cope with new business it has to have a total of 720m^2 of storage space. It currently has 450m^2 of space. By what percentage does its total storage space need to increase?

A: 55%

B: 70%

C: 45%

D: 60%

E: 75%

FRACTIONS, DECIMALS & PERCENTAGES

Work out the answer for the following questions and circle the correct answer from the multiple choices provided.

161.

What is 0.35 as a percentage?

A: 70%

B: 35%

C: 3.5%

D: 0.35%

E: 20%

162.

What is two fifths as a percentage?

A: 45%

B: 40%

C: 55%

D: 35%

E: 60%

163.

What is $^7/_{20}$ as a decimal?

A: 0.27

B: 0.42

C: 0.3

D: 0.35

E: 0.4

164.

What is 8 percent as a fraction?

A: $^1/_{13}$

B: $^1/_{12}$

C: $^1/_{15}$

D: $^3/_{25}$

E: $^2/_{25}$

Think Smart Academy ltd ©

165.

What is $^{21}/_{50}$ as a decimal?

A: 0.41

B: 0.45

C: 0.44

D: 0.40

E: 0.42

166.

What is 0.09 as a percentage?

A: 90%

B: 9%

C: 0.9%

D: 0.09%

E: 0.009%

167.

What is 0.025 as a percentage?

A: 0.25%

B: 2.5%

C: 0.025%

D: 25%

E: 0.0025%

168.

What is $^{3}/_{15}$ as a percentage?

A: 15%

B: 30%

C: 20%

D: 25%

E: 22.5%

169.

What is 6.6% as a decimal?

A: 0.066

B: 0.0066

C: 0.606

D: 0.66

E: 0.066

170.

What is $^6/_{125}$ as a decimal?

A: 0.55

B: 0.48

C: 0.048

D: 0.48

E: 0.055

171.

What is 35.5% as a fraction?

A: $^{66}/_{200}$

B: $^{77}/_{200}$

C: $^{66}/_{350}$

D: $^{45}/_{170}$

E: $^{71}/_{200}$

172.

What is $^{169}/_{200}$ as a decimal?

A: 0.845

B: 0.855

C: 0.085

D: 0.835

E: 0.825

173.

What is 67.09% as a decimal?

A: 0.06709

B: 0.67009

C: 0.6790

D: 0.6709

E: 0.679

174.

What is 5.7 - 4.9 as a percentage?

A: 8%

B: 80%

C: 90%

D: 9%

E: 82%

175.

What is $^5/_8$ as a percentage?

A: 64%

B: 61%

C: 62.5%

D: 63%

E: 65%

176.

What is $^2/_5$ + $^1/_5$ as a percentage?

A: 65%

B: 55%

C: 62%

D: 60%

E: 67%

177.

What is 0.025% as a decimal?

A: 0.00205

B: 0.025

C: 0.0025

D: 0.000025

E: 0.00025

178.

What is $\frac{3}{5}$ x $\frac{1}{2}$ as a percentage?

A: 30%

B: 40%

C: 35%

D: 0.3%

E: 32%

179.

What is 0.725 as a fraction?

A: $\frac{6}{10}$

B: $\frac{29}{40}$

C: $\frac{27}{40}$

D: $\frac{33}{55}$

E: $\frac{36}{50}$

180.

What is 4.04% as a decimal?

A: 0.404

B: 0.00404

C: 0.0404

D: 0.04004

E: 0.4004

QUESTION	ANSWER	QUESTION	ANSWER	QUESTION	ANSWER	QUESTION	ANSWER	QUESTION	ANSWER
1	71	41	B	81	A	121	B	161	B
2	103	42	C	82	E	122	D	162	B
3	99	43	A	83	C	123	B	163	D
4	125	44	D	84	D	124	C	164	E
5	169	45	C	85	B	125	C	165	E
6	608	46	A	86	A	126	A	166	B
7	372	47	D	87	E	127	A	167	B
8	945	48	B	88	D	128	E	168	C
9	2186	49	E	89	B	129	A	169	A
10	44162	50	C	90	B	130	C	170	C
11	16	51	E	91	D	131	E	171	E
12	29	52	A	92	A	132	E	172	A
13	38	53	E	93	A	133	D	173	D
14	13	54	B	94	C	134	A	174	B
15	58	55	E	95	A	135	C	175	C
16	144	56	B	96	D	136	D	176	D
17	249	57	A	97	A	137	A	177	E
18	588	58	C	98	D	138	A	178	A
19	649	59	C	99	B	139	D	179	B
20	1667	60	A	100	B	140	D	180	C
21	126	61	D	101	D	141	A		
22	80	62	C	102	C	142	C		
23	299	63	B	103	D	143	E		
24	385	64	B	104	B	144	C		
25	704	65	D	105	D	145	B		
26	2090	66	B	106	B	146	C		
27	2067	67	A	107	A	147	A		
28	17608	68	C	108	B	148	E		
29	25110	69	D	109	C	149	B		
30	55296	70	A	110	E	150	A		
31	14	71	E	111	C	151	B		
32	15	72	A	112	E	152	E		
33	39	73	D	113	A	153	B		
34	47	74	D	114	E	154	D		
35	29	75	A	115	A	155	B		
36	17	76	E	116	E	156	B		
37	19	77	D	117	B	157	E		
38	56	78	C	118	B	158	C		
39	22	79	A	119	A	159	A		
40	38	80	C	120	A	160	D		

Printed in Great Britain
by Amazon

22957510R00026